LITTLE BOOK
❦ OF ❦
DUCKS

WEIDENFELD & NICOLSON
LONDON

DUCKS

Feathered Friends

In what lies the fascination of ducks? For an overwhelming fascination it is, and one that grows and becomes more and more commanding. The very haunts of wild duck - the grey waters, open spaces and wild country, and the cold, rough weather that is most associated with them, exercise a particular charm which nothing else quite equals. The unforgettable thrill of evening flight when at dusk flocks of just discernible forms come wheeling in, whispering in conversation, as with the soft swish of wings they settle down on the pond they have chosen for the night, is met at the other extreme by the intense satisfaction of feeding and becoming friends with such intrinsically wild creatures when they have lost all fear of man and become condescending accepters of food from him.

A BOOK OF DUCKS
Phyllis Barclay-Smith

WATCHING THE DUCKS
Arthur Strachan 1865-1954

The Duck

Behold the duck.
It does not cluck.
A cluck it lacks.
It quacks.
It is especially fond
Of a puddle or a pond.
When it dines or sups,
It bottoms ups.

Ogden Nash
1 9 0 2 - 1 9 7 1

DUCKS

DUCKS ON THE RIVERBANK *Carl Jutz* 1835-1916

DUCKS

CHILDREN PLAYING WITH DUCKS
William Bromley 19th century

WINTER DUCKS

❉

Small in the shrink of winter, dark of the frost and chill,
Dawnlight beyond my window sill,
I lace the morning stiffly on my feet,
Print bootsteps down the snowy hill to meet
My ducks all waiting where the long black night
Has iced the pond around them. With a spade
I break the water clear; the hole I made
Restores their world to quacking rhyme and reason -
Tails up, they duck the lowering, grey-skied season,
Heads down, they listen to the still-warm song
Of silted leaves and summer, when the days were long.

Russell Hoban

DUCKS

The Wild Duck

Twilight. Red in the west.
Dimness. A glow on the wood.
The teams plod home to rest.
The wild duck come to glean.
O souls not understood,
What things have the farm ducks seen
That they cry so - huddle and cry?

Only the soul that goes.
Eager. Eager. Flying.
Over the globe of the moon,
Over the wood that glows.
Wings linked. Necks a-strain,
A rush and a wild crying.

A cry of long pain
In the reeds of a steel lagoon,
In a land that no man knows.

John Masefield
1878 - 1967

DUCKS IN FLIGHT

Edgar Hunt 1 8 7 6 - 1 9 5 3

Ducks' Ditty

All along the backwater,
Through the rushes tall,
Ducks are a-dabbling,
Up tails all!

Ducks' tails, drakes' tails,
Yellow feet a-quiver,
Yellow bills all out of sight
Busy in the river!

Slushy green undergrowth
Where the roach swim -
Here we keep our larder,
Cool and full and dim.

Everyone for what he likes!
We like to be
Heads down, tails up,
Dabbling free!

High in the blue above
Swifts whirl and call -
We are down a-dabbling,
Up tails all!

THE WIND IN THE WILLOWS
Kenneth Grahame 1859-1932

DUCKS AND DUCKLINGS ON A POND

Alexander Koester 1 8 6 4 - 1 9 3 2

DUCKS

DUCKS AND RABBITS

John Frederick Herring 1795-1865

A Foxy Tail

Jemima alighted rather heavily, and began to waddle about in search of a convenient dry nesting-place. She rather fancied a tree-stump amongst some tall fox-gloves.

But – seated upon the stump, she was startled to find an elegantly dressed gentleman reading a newspaper.

He had black prick ears and sandy coloured whiskers . . .

Jemima thought him mighty civil and handsome. She explained that she had not lost her way, but that she was trying to find a convenient dry nesting-place.

'. . . I have a sackful of feathers in my woodshed. No, my dear Madam, you will be in nobody's way. You may sit there as long as you like,' said the bushy long-tailed gentleman.

He said he loved eggs and ducklings; he should be proud to see a fine nestful in his wood-shed.

THE TALE OF JEMIMA PUDDLE-DUCK

Beatrix Potter 1866-1943

DUCKS

THE MALLARD

Brown-checked, neat as new
  spring tweed,
A mallard, wing-stretched
  in the sun,
Watched from the back of
  a beer-bubble stream
Her ducklings, one after one,
Daring, dipping in
  dazzling weed,
Nuzzling joyful mud.
Black and yellow, downy
  as bees,
They busied about a fringe
  of reed
In a paddled nursery pool.

The mother, content, lay dry,
Relaxed her wings, slackened
  her throat,
Dared to close one
  bead-black eye
When swift as terror a
  lightening stoat
Forked and flashed upstream.

Splatter and splash of
  mother and young -
Feathered drops whirled in
  a storm of fear,
Water thrashed in flight.
A stone for the stoat -
  I flung it near
And stood alone, not
  knowing what fate
Lay crouched in wait, while
  the stillness there
Grew ominous and bright.

Phoebe Hesketh

OUT FOR A SWIM

Georg Mesmer early 20th century

DUCKS

A True Blue Gentleman

This gentleman the charming duck
Quack quack says he
My tail's on
Fire, but he's only kidding

You can tell that
By his grin
He's one big grin, from wobbly
Feet to wobbly tail
Quack quack he tells us

Tail's on fire again

Ah yes
This charming gentleman the duck
With
His quaint alarms and
Trick of walking like a
Drunken hat
Quack quack says he

There's your fried egg.

Kenneth Patchen

DUCKS

THE FAMILY

Harry Bright 19th century

A MEMORY

Four ducks on a pond,
A grass-bank beyond,
A blue sky of spring,
White clouds on the wing:
What a little thing
To remember for years -
To remember with tears.

NIGHTINGALE VALLEY
William Allingham 1828-1889

MOTHER DUCK WITH DUCKLINGS IN THE WATER

David Adolph Constant Artz 1837-1890

DUCKS

In Sickness And In Health

The Muscovy drake had arrived in a sack brought in the back of a car by a young farmer who aimed to make himself popular with the Wyllie family. He could not have created a worse impression. Jane, Jeremy and their mother would have starved rather than eat it . . .

'And what, Jane,' I asked, 'is the procedure for looking after a Muscovy drake?' . . .

'Oh, it's quite simple,' said Jane, talking to me as if I were a backward small boy, 'it'll be quite all right in the chicken run with Hetty.' Hetty was our one remaining chicken . . .

The drake and Hetty developed a strong, platonic attachment and when Hetty, due to old age, began to fade away, the attention of the drake was touching to watch. For the last two days of her life he never left her side. They remained together in the chicken-house refusing to come out. Nor could he be tempted to eat anything.

A DRAKE AT THE DOOR
Derek Tangye

DUCKS

A BOY WITH POULTRY AND A GOAT
IN A FARMYARD
Edgar Hunt 1876 - 1953

DUCKS

MALLARD RISING, WINTER
Archibald Thorburn 1860-1935

DUCKS

THE WILD DUCK

WILD DUCK,
or MALLARD

As boys where playing in their schools dislike
And floating paper boats along the dyke
They laid their baskets down a nest to see
And found a small hole in a hollow tree
When one looked in and wonder filled his breast
And halloed out a wild duck on her nest
They doubted and the boldest went before
And the duck bolted when they waded o'er
And suthied up and flew against the wind
And left the boys and wondering thoughts behind
The eggs lay hid in down and lightly prest
They counted more than thirty in the nest
They filled their hats with eggs and wader o'er
And left the nest as quiet as before.

John Clare 1 7 9 3 - 1 8 6 4

Comical Creatures

From troubles of the world
I turn to ducks,
Beautiful comical things
Sleeping or curled
Their heads beneath white wings
By water cool,
Or finding curious things
To eat in various mucks
Beneath the pool,
Tails uppermost, or waddling
Sailor-like on the shores
Of ponds, or paddling
- Left! right! - with fanlike feet
Which are for steady oars
When they (white galleys) float
Each bird a boat
Rippling at will the sweet
Wide waterway . . .

DUCKS
Frederick William Harvey 1 8 8 8 - 1 9 5 7

DUCKS

DUCKS PREENING
Franz Grassel 19th century

DUCKS

DILLY, DILLY!

Around a roadside pond halfway up the village street stand old pollarded willows, the trunks hollowed by time to mere shells in which the village children hide, but every tree with its living topknot of silvery green leaves. A few white Aylesbury ducks still frequent this pond, though not so many as in former years, when, towards nightfall, little girls with light switches in their hands would go to the pond to call in those belonging to their families. '*Dilly, dilly, dilly, dilly!* ' they would call, and the ducks would scramble up the bank and, with many a backward glance from their cunning little eyes, they would form two files and waddle off, one file up and the other down the street. It was as the children said, hard to tell which was whosen; but the ducks knew to whom they belonged. In twos and threes they would break rank and make for the garden gate which led to the shed where they knew they would find in their troughs a delicious mess of mashed potatoes and brewer's grain.

STILL GLIDES THE STREAM
Flora Thompson 1876-1947

DUCKS

THE LAMBOURN VALLEY,
BERKSHIRE, EAST GARSTON VILLAGE
David Hewitt early 20th century

27

DUCKS

TO A WATERFOWL

DUCKS *Thomas Armstrong 1835-1911*

Whither, 'midst falling dew,
While glow the heavens with the last steps of day,
Far, through their rosy depths, dost thou pursue
Thy solitary way!

Vainly the fowler's eye
Might mark thy distant flight to do thee wrong,
As, darkly painted on the crimson sky,
Thy figure floats along.

Seek'st thou the plashy brink
Of weedy lake, or marge of river wide,
Or where the rocking billows rise and sink
On the chafed ocean side?

DUCKS

There is a power whose care
Teaches thy way along that pathless coast, -
The desert and illimitable air, -
Lone wandering, but not lost.

All day thy wings have fanned,
At that far height, the cold, thin atmosphere,
Yet stoop not, weary, to the welcome land,
Though the dark night is near.

And soon that toil shall end;
Soon shalt thou find a summer home, and rest,
And scream among thy fellows; reeds shall bend,
Soon, o'er thy sheltered nest.

Thou'rt gone, the abyss of heaven
Hath swallowed up thy form; yet, on my heart
Deeply hath sunk the lesson thou hast given,
And shall not soon depart.

He who, from zone to zone,
Guides through the boundless sky thy certain flight,
In the long way that I must tread alone,
Will lead my steps aright.

William Cullen Bryant 1794-1878

DUCKS

An annual invasion

TAMED in his enclosures were the geese that came winging down the coast from Iceland and Spitzbergen each October, in great skeins that darkened the sky and filled the air with the rushing noise of their passage - the brown-bodied pink-feet, white-breasted barnacles, with their dark necks and clowns' masks, the wild white fronts with black-barred breasts, and many species of wild ducks - widgeon, mallard, pintails, teal and shovellers . . .

Rhayader was content in the knowledge that when storms blew, or it was bitter cold and food was scarce, or the big punt guns of the distant bag hunters roared, his birds were safe; that he had gathered to the sanctuary and security of his own arms and heart these many wild and beautiful creatures who knew and trusted him.

They would answer the call of the north in the spring, but in the fall they would come back, barking and whooping and honking in the autumn sky, to circle the landmark of the old light and drop to earth near by to be his guest again - birds that he well remembered and recognized from the previous year.

THE SNOW GOOSE
Paul Gallico 1897-1976

DUCK RISING
Archibald Thorburn 1860-1935

FEEDING
THE DUCKS
Frans Van Holder
1 8 8 1 - 1 9 1 9

DUCKS

REGRETS

I walked one day in a Kentish park
To hear some sweet bird's notes,
But every blackcap, linnet and lark
Had a choke that day in his throat.
And while each one with a drooping wing
Was wiping a tear from his eye
I heard a sad, sad lady sing
From the edge of a pond close by:
'O Carolina! O my duck!
O Carolin, my dear!
My pretty little pond has lost its luck
Now you're no longer here.'

THE COUNTRY WALK
Sir Henry John Newbolt 1 8 6 2 - 1 9 3 8

DUCKS

QUACK!

The duck is whiter than whey is,
   His tail tips up over his back,
The eye in his head is as round as a button,
   And he says, *Quack! Quack!*

He swims on his bright blue mill-pond,
   By the willow tree under the shack,
Then he stands on his head to see down to the bottom,
   And says, *Quack! Quack!*

When Mollie steps out of the kitchen,
   For apron - pinned round with a sack;
He squints at her round face, her dish, and what's in it,
   And says, *Quack! Quack!*

He preens the pure snow of his feathers
   In the sun by the wheat-straw stack;
At dusk waddles home with his brothers and sisters,
   And says, *Quack! Quack!*

Walter de la Mare 1873 - 1956

DUCKS

THE MILL STREAM

Charles Edward Wilson early 20th century

DUCKS

DUCK CHASING

———— ✳ ————

I spied a very small brown duck
Riding the swells of the sea
Like a rocking-chair. 'Little duck!'
I cried. I paddled away,
I paddled after it. When it dived,
Down I dived: too smoky was the sea,
We were lost. It surfaced
In the west, I torpedoed west
And when it dived I dived,
And we were lost and lost and lost
In the slant smoke of the sea.
When I came floating up on it
From the side, like a deadman,
And yelled suddenly, it took off,
It skimmed the swells as it ascended,
Brown wings burning and flashing
In the sun as the sea it rose over
Burned and flashed underneath it.
I did not see the little duck again.
Duck-chasing is a game like any game.
When it is over it is all over.

Gallway Kinnell

LONG-TAILED DUCK

Archibald Thorburn 1860-1935

DUCKS

WATER BIRDS
Roman Mosaic 1st century AD

DUCKS

The Prayer
of the Little Ducks

Dear God,
Give us a flood of water.
Let it rain tomorrow and always.
Give us plenty of little slugs
and other luscious things to eat.
Protect all folk who quack
And everyone who knows how to swim.
Amen.

PRAYERS FROM THE ARK
Carmen Bernos de Gasztold,
translated by Rumer Godden

The Ugly Duckling

It was summertime; the wheat was golden, the oats were green and the hay piled high in the meadows. In a quiet, sunny spot near the farmyard, a duck sat nesting, impatiently waiting for the last of her eggs to hatch.

At last, the final egg cracked and to the mother's dismay out tumbled a huge, ugly, grey duckling. The mother tried to hide her horror and took the unsightly creature up to the farm along with its brothers and sisters.

The other animals stared at the ugly duckling and whispered horrible things. They were so cruel that the poor duckling fled the farm in tears. His life became a miserable, lonely struggle to survive.

One day, he saw the most beautiful birds imaginable gliding across a pond. One let out a single note that filled the duckling's melancholy breast with a strange yearning. He swam towards the beautiful swans. As he did so, he noticed his reflection in the water. He was no longer an ugly grey duckling - he had become a beautiful swan.

Hans Christian Andersen 1805-1875

A HAPPY FAMILY

Norbert Schrodl 1842 - 1912

The Whistle of Wings

STANDING in the great stone-flagged kitchen, lit by the red glow of the charcoal fires, he explained how the flock of ducks had come over in the wintry dawn, spread out across the sky. With a shrill whistle of wings they had swept overhead, and Leslie had picked out the leader, fired, turned his gun on to the second bird, and fired again with terrific speed, so that when he lowered his barrels the two ducks splashed into the lake almost as one. Gathered in the kitchen, the family listened spellbound to his graphic description. The broad wooden table was piled high with game, Mother and Margo were plucking a brace of ducks for dinner, I was examining the various species and making notes on them in my diary (which was rapidly becoming more bloodstained and feather-covered), and Larry was sitting on a chair, a neat, dead mallard in his lap, stroking its crisp wings and watching, as Leslie, up to the waist in an imaginary swamp, for the third time showed us how he achieved his left-and-a-right.

MY FAMILY AND OTHER ANIMALS
Gerald Durrell

DUCKS

FOWLING SCENE

19th century

The Duck and the Kangaroo

Said the Duck to the Kangaroo,
'Good gracious! how you hop!
Over the fields and the water too,
As if you never would stop!
My life is a bore in this nasty pond,
And I long to go out in the world beyond!
I wish I could hop like you!'
Said the Duck to the Kangaroo.

'Please give me a ride on your back!'
Said the Duck to the Kangaroo.
'I would sit quite still, and say nothing but "Quack",
The whole of the long day through!
And we'd go to the Dee, and the Jelly Bo Lee,
Over the land, and over the sea; -
Please take me a ride! O do!'
Said the Duck to the Kangaroo.

DUCKS

Said the Kangaroo to the Duck,
'This requires some little reflection;
Perhaps on the whole it might bring me luck,
And there seems but one objection,
Which is, if you'll let me speak so bold,
Your feet are unpleasantly wet and cold,
And would probably give me the roo-
Matiz! said the Kangaroo.

Said the Duck, 'As I sat on the rocks,
I thought over that completely,
And I bought four pairs of worsted socks
Which fit my web-feet neatly.
And to keep out the cold I've bought a cloak,
And every day a cigar I'll smoke,
All to follow my own dear true
Love of a Kangaroo!'

Said the Kangaroo, 'I'm ready!
All in the moonlight pale;
But to balance me well, dear Duck, sit steady!
And quite at the end of my tail!'
So away they went with a hop and a bound,
And they hopped the whole world three times round;
And who so happy, - O who,
As the Duck and the Kangaroo?

Edward Lear 1812 - 1888

THE DUCK

I hope you may have better luck
Than to be bitten by the duck.

This bird is generally tame,
But he is dangerous all the same;

And though he looks so small and weak,
He has a very powerful beak.

Between the hours of twelve and two
You never know what he may do.

And sometimes he plays awkward tricks
From half-past four to half-past six.

And any hour of the day
It's best to keep out of his way.

Lord Alfred Douglas
1870-1945

A CONFRONTATION
Minna Stocks early 20th century

DUCKS

The Wild Duck's Nest

THE IMPERIAL CONSORT of the Fairy-king
Owns not a sylvan bower; or gorgeous cell
With emerald floored, and with purpureal shell
Ceilinged and roofed; that is so fair a thing
As this low structure, for the tasks of spring
Prepared by one who loves the buoyant swell
Of the brisk waves, yet here consents to dwell;
And spreads in steadfast peace her brooding wing.
Words cannot paint the o'ershadowing yew-tree bough,
And dimly-gleaming nest, - a hollow crown
Of golden leaves inlaid with silver down,
Fine as the mother's softest plumes allow:
I gazed - and, self-accused while gazing, sighed
For human kind, weak slaves of cumbrous pride!

William Wordsworth 1770-1850

DUCKS

DUCKS AND DRAKES ON A ROCKY BANK
Alexander Koester 1864-1932

DUCKS

A SUMMER'S DAY *James Mackay* 19th century

DUCKS

DINNER DUCKS

Oh, what have you got for dinner, Mrs Bond?
There's beef in the larder, and ducks in the pond;
Dilly, dilly, dilly, dilly, come to be killed,
For you must be stuffed and my customers filled!

  Send us the beef first, good Mrs Bond,
  And get us some ducks dressed out of the pond,
  Cry, Dilly, dilly, dilly, come to be killed,
  For you must be stuffed and my customers filled!

John Ostler, go fetch me a duckling or two.
Ma'am, says John Ostler, I'll try what I can do.
Cry, Dilly, dilly, dilly, come to be killed,
For you must be stuffed and my customers filled!

  I have been to the ducks that swim in the pond,
  But I found they won't come to be killed, Mrs Bond;
  I cried, Dilly, dilly, dilly, dilly, come to be killed,
  For you must be stuffed and my customers filled!

TRADITIONAL

DUCKS

FIRST LOVE

uaggy was one of these, a tiny mallard duckling which some boys had rescued from a dog. He was unharmed but badly shocked. I put him in a hay-lined box with a hot-water bottle and installed him in a cupboard. I knew that if he could get through the night he had a good chance of survival, so next morning I was delighted to see that he was not only alive but noisily demanding his breakfast . . .

When mating time came around, he suffered an identity crisis. For one thing, he hadn't seen another duck since babyhood and probably didn't even know he was a duck. For another, he identified more closely with me than with any other creature. As the part of me he had most contact with was my feet, he fell madly in love with my wellies. He displayed to them, he courted them and he did his utmost to mate with them. Callers got used to seeing me hobbling around with a besotted duck firmly attached to my foot.

ALL THE BEASTS OF THE FIELD
Sylvia Fenton

DUCKS

A SPRING IDYLL

Charles Whitworth 19th century

DUCKS

Daddy Fell into the Pond

Everyone grumbled. The sky was grey.
We had nothing to do and nothing to say.
We were nearing the end of a dismal day,
And there seemed to be nothing beyond,
Then
Daddy fell into the pond!

And everyone's face grew merry and bright,
And Timothy danced for sheer delight.
'Give me the camera, quick, oh quick!
He's crawling out of the duckweed.' *Click!*

Then the gardener suddenly slapped his knee,
And he doubled up, shaking silently,
And the ducks all quacked as if they were daft
And it sounded as if the old drake laughed.

O, there wasn't a thing that didn't respond
When
Daddy fell into the pond!

Alfred Noyes 1880-1958

DUCKS

A c k n o w l e d g e m e n t s

Designed and edited by
THE BRIDGEWATER BOOK COMPANY
Words and Pictures chosen by
RHODA NOTTRIDGE
Typesetting by VANESSA GOOD
Printed in Italy

*The publishers wish to thank the following
for the use of pictures:*
THE BRIDGEMAN ART LIBRARY: pages 5, 9,
19, 21; MARY EVANS PICTURE LIBRARY: page 44;
E.T. ARCHIVE: pages 38, 43; FINE ART
PHOTOGRAPHS: front and back cover and pages 3, 6,
11, 12, 15, 17, 22, 25, 27, 28, 31, 32, 35, 37, 41, 47,
49, 50, 53, 54.

*The publishers gratefully acknowledge permission to
reproduce the following material in this book:*
p.2 *A Book of Ducks* by Phyllis Barclay-Smith published
by Penguin Books Ltd © 1951, reproduced by
permission of Penguin Books Ltd.
p.4 *The Duck* by Ogden Nash from IWouldn''t Have
Missed It by permission Andre Deutsch Ltd.
p.7 *Winter Ducks* by Russell Hoban from The Pedalling
Man published by Heinemann Ltd by permission David
Higham Associates Ltd.
p.8 *The Wild Duck* by John Masefield by permission
The Society of Authors as the literary representative of
the Estate of John Masefield.
p.13 From *The Tale of Jemima Puddle-Duck* by Beatrix
Potter, copyright © Frederick Warne & Co., 1908,1987.

p. 14 *The Mallard* by Phoebe Hesketh by permission
HarperCollins.
p.16 *A True Blue Gentleman* by Kenneth Patcham
from Collected Poems. Copyright 1952 by Kenneth
Patchen, reprinted by permission of New Directions
Publishing Corp.
p.20 *A Drake At The Door* by Derek Tangye (Michael
Joseph, 1972) copyright © Derek Tangye, 1972 and by
permission Laurence Pollinger (USA).
p.24 Extract from Ducks by Frederick William Harvey
by permission Sidgwick & Jackson.
p.26 *Still Glides The Stream* by Flora Thompson,
Oxford University Press 1948 by permission of
Oxford University Press.
p.30 *The Snow Goose* by Paul Gallico, copyright © 1941
the Estate of the late Paul Gallico by permission Aitken
& Stone Ltd.
p.34 *Quack!* by Walter de la Mare by permission The
Literary Trustees of Walter de la Mare and The Society
of Authors as their representative.
p.36 *Duck Chasing* from What A Kingdom It Was by
Galway Kinnell. Copyright © 1960, © renewed 1988 by
Galway Kinnell. Reprinted by permission of Houghton
Mifflin Co. All rights reserved.
p.39 *The Prayer of the Little Ducks* from Prayers From
The Ark by Carmen Bernos de Gasztold, translated by
Rumer Godden by permission Pan MacMillan
Children's Books.
p.42 *My Family and Other Animals* by Gerald Durrell by
permission Penguin Viking.
p.46 *The Duck* by Lord Alfred Douglas from Tails with
a Twist, reproduced by permission Sheila Colman,
executor of the Lord Alfred Douglas Literary Estate.
p.52 *All The Beasts of the Field* by Sylvia Fenton,
HarperCollins.
p.55 *Daddy Fell into the Pond* by Alfred Noyes from
Selected Poems by permission John Murrray
(Publishers) Ltd.

*Every effort has been made to trace all
copyright holders and obtain permissions.
The editor and publishers sincerely
apologise for any inadvertent errors or
omissions and will be happy to correct
them in any future edition.*